With Bonus Material from
the Obama White House,
Democratic Congress,
and Other Special Friends!

Sh★t My
Vice President Says

Threshold Editions

New York London Toronto Sydney

Threshold Editions
A Division of Simon & Schuster, Inc.
1230 Avenue of the Americas
New York, NY 10020

First Threshold Editions trade paperback edition December 2010

THRESHOLD EDITIONS and colophon are trademarks of Simon & Schuster, Inc.

For information about special discounts for bulk purchases, please contact
Simon & Schuster Special Sales at 1-866-506-1949 or
business@simonandschuster.com.

The Simon & Schuster Speakers Bureau can bring authors to your live event.
For more information or to book an event contact the Simon & Schuster Speakers
Bureau at 1-866-248-3049 or visit our website at www.simonspeakers.com.

Designed by Ruth Lee-Mui

Manufactured in the United States of America

10 9 8 7 6 5 4 3 2 1

Library of Congress Cataloging-in-Publication Data

Sh*t my vice president says : with bonus material from the Obama White House,
Democratic Congress, and other special friends!—1st Threshold Editions trade pbk. ed.
   p.   cm.
Includes bibliographical references.
1. United States—Politics and government—2009—Humor. 2. Obama, Barack—Humor.
3. Biden, Joseph R.—Humor. 4. Presidents—United States—Humor. 5. Vice Presidents—
United States—Humor. 6. Legislators—United States—Humor. 7. United States.
Congress—Humor. 8. American wit and humor. I. Title: Shit my vice-president says.
E907.S44 2010
973.932—dc22   2010047175

ISBN 978-1-4516-2763-3
ISBN 978-1-4516-2772-5 (ebook)

For my grandmother, Madelyn Dunham.
Although you were a typical white person who
once confessed your fear of black men,
I don't hold that against you.

—B.O.

Contents

Introduction:
Why I Had to Write This Book

They say the best offense is a good defense.

With my poll numbers in a nosedive and with the 2012 election just around the corner, I've decided to take off the gloves and come out swinging to defend myself. From whom, you ask? This might surprise you, but with friends like Joe Biden and other dimwit Democrats in Congress and on my staff, who needs enemies? Let's start with my veep.

Look, I have nothing personally against Joe Biden.

Really. I don't. Aside from the fact that he's been a complete pain in my ass ever since my campaign advisors insisted we put him on the ticket. At the time, I told them I'd prefer to run with an African-American over Joe Biden. You know, somebody I knew *personally* and could trust—like my pastor, Reverend Jeremiah Wright.

Having spent twenty years listening to Reverend Wright, I can attest he's f——king brilliant. He has such insight into public policy. Like the time in church when he told us, "The government lied about inventing the HIV virus as a means of genocide against people of color."[1]

You're not gonna find that sort of analysis in the mainstream press.

My advisors, however, argued with Joe Biden we'd get more mileage out of that whole "ebony and ivory" motif that Stevie Wonder and

Paul McCartney sang about. Plus, they said Joe had a certain Hugh Hefner look-alike appeal that'd be popular with the young female voters. While conceding the point, I told them that I was still stewing over Joe's dig against me that "the presidency is not something that lends itself to on-the-job-training."[2]

As it's turned out, no amount of training has kept Joe's mouth from insulting Indian-Americans, the disabled, and hardworking entrepreneurs—which I document thoroughly in this book. No question, the guy's a walking gaffe machine on steroids. Hell, he even screws up his own history. Joe claimed he graduated "in the top half" of his class at Syracuse College of Law. He'd be right . . . IF graduating seventy-sixth out of a class of eighty-five students qualified as the top half. Let's set aside his claim that he "graduated with three degrees from college"[3] when in reality it was one.

Who's counting, right?

To be honest, if I had to go with a Caucasian running mate, my first choice would have been my old friend Bill Ayers. He and I were tight back in Chicago. Bill loved the idea. We both knew, however, there was no easy way to put a positive spin on some of the stuff he's said and done along the way.

Take that little matter of Bill's fascination with terrorism and explosives. Or the fact that Bill once said, "Everything was absolutely ideal on the day I bombed the Pentagon . . . the sky was blue. The birds were singing. And the bastards were finally going to get what was coming to them."[4] Nope. Even Bill Clinton with his unmatched ability to parse words couldn't spin that.

So I got stuck with Joe.

In spite of having a nimrod of a vice president, we won the 2008 election with my message of hope and change. You see, voters were unhappy with the direction of the country. I was, too. George Bush trashed America with his fiscal policies, which favored his rich cronies. He evidently lost sight of the core values espoused by one of our Founding Fathers, Karl Marx, who taught that we must spread the wealth around.

That's what I promised, and that's what I've been doing these first two years.

After all, when you spread the wealth around it's a good thing for everybody.

At the same time, from the moment I arrived in the White House, I found myself surrounded by idiots. I'm the eighth U.S. president with a Harvard degree. I'm smart. I'm "clean" (as Joe pointed out). And I'm nothing if I'm not articulate, especially when near a tele-prompter. Look, I know what I'm doing. My Democratic associates on the Hill, however, have let me down. They routinely say and do some of the dumbest things. These gaffes are a distraction from my mission and have compromised my ability to lead.

I wrote this book to chronicle a number of those blunders on their part.

Why? That way you'll know whom to toss out of office in 2012.

Let me be clear. There are those who claim I've said my share of whoppers. My enemies on the right are quick to point out the time when I said on the campaign trail, "Over the last fifteen months, we've traveled to every corner of the United States. I've now been in fifty-seven states? I think there's one left to go."

Look. I am not a newcomer to this. I *know* there are fifty states—so far.

But why stop there?

I'm a visionary. I'm not stuck in the past. All I was doing was projecting into the future, to a time when our flag might proudly be expanded to include new states. In fact, I'm no different from that great philosopher John Lennon, who sang, "Imagine there's no countries / It isn't hard to do / Nothing to kill or die for." I remember smoking weed listening to that tune, envisioning a day when flags and borders won't be necessary. He's right, they're so divisive.

Which is why I once told the president of Mexico, "In the twenty-first century, we are not defined by our borders, but by our bond."[5]

So, welcome to the New America. Or, in the words of my secretary of state, Hillary Clinton, "God bless the America we are trying to create."[6]

There's still much to be done. Where do we start?

Vote for me in 2012 . . . and toss out the deadweight exemplified herein.

—B.O.

CHAPTER 1

What's in a Name?

It's no secret that my name has become a political football ever since I campaigned for the presidency. Obviously, when my parents named me they never imagined I'd run for president.

I mean, what are the odds that the last name of the dictator we just overthrew and my middle name—Hussein—would be the same? Talk about your tough luck! (What if Harry Truman's middle name had been Hitler?)

To top it off, my first name isn't a word that most Americans have ever heard of. Let's be clear: It's unlikely that "Barack" ever topped the Most Popular Baby Names list in this country. Not to mention how some of those BIRTHER people can't have enough fun with the fact that "Obama" rhymes with "Osama." Everybody's a comedian, right?

So, with all this name baggage, you can see how important it was that I be introduced properly on official occasions. David Axelrod and my other consultants thought this was especially true at the start of the campaign.

As soon as we had picked Joe Biden for my running mate in the '08 election, we scheduled a rally in Springfield, Illinois—my home state. That, of course, is the home of Abe Lincoln, Rod Blagojevich, and so on.

At the time, it made sense to entrust my introduction to Joe Biden. After all, as vice president he wouldn't have *that* much to do. Why not let him start off by making sure people heard my name correctly.

That was the plan. Here's what happened . . .

"This election year the choice is clear! One man stands ready to deliver change we desperately need. A man I'm proud to call my friend. A man who will be the next president of the United States . . . Barack America!!"

—Joe Biden, August 23, 2008[7]

CHAPTER 2

My Resident Smart-ass

No, I'm not talking about Michelle.

Although, come to think of it, I've often thought . . . wait a sec—
I better not go there. When it comes to resident smart-asses I'm talk-
ing about my veep. The guy's a walking gaffe machine with a set of
Energizer lithium batteries that keep on going.

Just the other day I sent Biden to Milwaukee for what *should* have
been a piece-of-cake assignment: to stump for Democratic senator
Russ Feingold. You see, Russ was having some difficulty with his
re-election bid even though he's as progressive as they come. Hell,
Russ voted against the Iraq War, he's been against the Patriot Act,
and, uh, he voted against bailing out Wall Street.

Even though he's a three-term incumbent, Russ was way behind
in the polls due to the Bush recession. Sensing that Russ could use
a little boost, I sent Joe to the rescue—you know, shake some hands,
read a prepared speech about how great I am for the country, and
then head to Kopp's Frozen Custard shop to snap photos with the
locals. What could be easier?

Leave it to Joe to flub such a simple mission.

He actually walked into a *custard* shop and asked for *ice cream*.

Nice, Joe. At least he offered to pay, I'll give him that much. The
manager, in turn, offered the custard to Joe for free, saying, "Don't
worry, it's on us. Lower our taxes and we'll call it even."

It all fell apart when Joe said . . .

"Why don't you say something nice instead of being a smart-ass all the time?"

—Joe Biden[8]

CHAPTER 3

You Must Be High

The White House received a package today from the California Medical Marijuana Retailers Association. It was addressed to me. I think they sent it as a gift for my forty-ninth birthday. My secretary, Katie Johnson, knew better than to put it on my desk in the Oval Office.

Couldn't risk a photo of that going out on the wire services, now could I?

I'm pretty sure Katie hid it behind the podium in the White House Press Briefing Room. Why do I say that?

Well, look. Everybody knows that the economy has been a disaster since I've been in office. I mean, for the past two years, housing starts are down more than 40 percent, the one-year Treasury rate is off nearly 90 percent, unemployment is up 57 percent, and the Dow Jones is down 9 percent. Even Ray Charles (may he rest in peace) could see that my approval ratings are in the toilet, one stall over from the toilet where the economy's numbers are swirling down the drain.

So why do I think my secretary hid the marijuana gift box in the Press Briefing Room podium?

Because my White House press secretary, Robert Gibbs, *had* to be smoking *something* when he made this statement to the press from behind that podium . . .

"By virtually any measure, our economy is in a better place than it was two years ago."

—Robert Gibbs, White House press secretary[9]

CHAPTER 4

Good Vibrations

I was sitting at a diner in South Bend, Indiana, sipping watered-down orange juice, pretending to listen to the locals as they carped about the lack of jobs, the down economy, and the mess Bush made of the country. Since Bill Clinton got a lot of political mileage out of milking the "everyman" approach, I figured I'd try my hand at hanging out with the average Joes.

Now, I realize this is a family book, so I need to be delicate here.

I mean, what happened was a bit of a shocker.

You see, I had just presented my ideas for a stimulus package and we were about to head to the next campaign stop. That's when one of the waitresses asked for a photograph together with me. Fine. I put my arm around her shoulder and leaned in next to her for the shot. We were so close that our legs were touching. That's when my pants started to vibrate. I mean, it really went *nuts*.

I felt it, and by the starry look in her eyes, she felt it, too.

Admittedly I have, uh, quite the *package*, but I assure you it wasn't *stimulated* at the time. Nothing against older women, but this gal had to be sixty; she most assuredly wasn't doing anything for me, if you know what I mean.

I certainly didn't want her to think I was getting a rise out of meeting her.

I didn't want her telling her friends that I was some kind of perv.

I knew I had to say something. While it wasn't exactly what you'd expect a presidential hopeful to say, I blurted out the first thing that came to mind . . .

"That's my phone buzzing there. I don't want you to think I'm getting fresh or anything."

—Me[10]

CHAPTER 5

Stinking Tourists

It's no secret that I'm not a fan of the Tea Party movement.

Although they're entitled to their sophomoric viewpoint, I think they're little more than a naïve, misled pack of zombies who spend far too much time listening to the hate speech spewed by the likes of Rush Limbaugh, Sean Hannity, Michael Savage, and Glenn Beck.

Anyway, it's one thing for these uptight tea-baggers (who clearly have no appreciation for all that I'm doing to fundamentally transform America) to hold their tedious, flag-waving rallies in flyover country. It's quite another thing to come to Washington, D.C., where these families block traffic, fill up trash cans with dirty diapers, and disturb those of us who are working hard to rule America.

Why, just the other day, although I was busy making a sandwich for the kids' lunches and didn't see it, I'm told a few hundred thousand unhappy Americans descended on the Capital Plaza for something called the "Restoring Honor" rally. While I had heard that they covered the National Mall like ants at a picnic, the fact of the matter is that I could actually *smell* them.

What's more, I remember saying to Harry Reid, "Harry, what's that awful smell? Did you rip one?" You know how old guys are. They're known for launching SBDs—"silent but deadly" gas. He said, "No, sir, those are tourists." Now, it's one thing to have a private conversation about stinking tourists. It's quite another thing to be saying something in public, as Harry decided to do . . .

"My staff tells me not to say this, but I'm going to say it anyway, in the summer because of the heat and high humidity, you could literally smell the tourists coming into the Capitol. It may be descriptive but it's true."

—Harry Reid, Democrat Senate majority leader[11]

CHAPTER 6

The Trouble with Spin

Admittedly, my economic plan is tanking faster than the ratings at CNN. And because of it, some are saying I'll go down in history as being worse than Jimmy Carter. They better not count me out. I understand the art of spin. I love spin. And with the media firmly in my corner, spinning a mess into a victory is as easy as luring Britney Spears into your apartment with a beer and a bag of cheese fries.

So, with an open bar brought into the Oval Office, my staff and I discussed how we'd turn these economic lemons into lemonade. We giggled as we talked about how we'd say, "Sure, we lost 18 bazillion jobs, but we *would* have lost 19 bazillion! We saved a bazillion jobs!" We laughed out loud as we imagined the headlines announcing, "A second Great Depression was Averted. Long live Obama!"

At times like that, I just love my job. We say it, the media spits it out as news. Sometime they elaborate to make my case even better.

I just wish I could get them all in one room and give them a big hug. Who am I kidding? I've done that about ten times already. I love these guys. They love me. We're family. Yes, I have an unparalleled advantage over truth.

Imagine my frustration, then, when Joe Biden popped his head out of his hole long enough to say the one thing even the media couldn't spin. How could one man so ignorantly screw up two historical facts to such an enormous degree? I mean, television wasn't around when Franklin D. Roosevelt was alive, nor was Roosevelt president when the stock market crashed.

That didn't stop Joe from saying

"When the stock market crashed, Franklin D. Roosevelt got on the television and didn't just talk about the, you know, the princes of greed. He said, 'Look, here's what happened.'"

—Joe Biden[12]

CHAPTER 7

Michelle's America

As I type this, I'm already having second thoughts. I really should tear this page up before my wife sees it. You see, Michelle is sleeping in the other room. This is about her. That, as you can imagine, can be dangerous. She doesn't wear those tiger-print outfits just for show.

For the record, I try to keep my family out of the public eye, unless I need them to further my cause or make a point. So, let's say about half the time they're great props for my purposes.

Hang on, here she comes. I need to come up with something sweet to say. Where the hell is my teleprompter?!!

Okay, she was too tired to notice what I'm doing. Just a quick, bleary-eyed trip to the restroom. Crisis averted. She's back in her bed.

Here's where I'm going with this: I believe I should get some kind of humanitarian award for becoming president even though my wife nearly snatched it from my hands.

I spent countless hours poring over those damn YouTube videos of Reverend Jeremiah Wright, desperately seeking a spin that would silence the critics. But what I failed to do was to train my own wife. Don't get me wrong. I did cover the basics: You will garden. You will talk about education. You will not snarl at voters. You will dress hot—but not *too* hot.

She agreed to all of that.

But here's my mistake. I didn't know I needed to tell her, "Honey, act like you actually *like* America." That's why in an unguarded moment she said . . .

"For the first time in my adult lifetime, I'm really proud of my country."

—Michelle Obama[13]

CHAPTER 8

I See Dead People

I should have known it was going to be one of those days.

I'm talking about May 26, 2008, Memorial Day.

At the time we'd been on the campaign trail for several weeks in a row. We were somewhere in New Mexico. I was pissed because I wanted to play a round of golf but my campaign manager, David Plouffe, had committed me to speak at some little Memorial Day commemorative thingy out in the freakin' desert with folding chairs and people waving little flags.

Michelle, who is ever concerned about the need to eat right, whipped up one of her "special shakes"—which is about as thick and tasty as fifty-weight motor oil. All I wanted to eat was my waffles. To keep the peace I jugged it down. She claimed her concoction would help my memory and keep me, uh, keep me from faltering when I, uh, speak. She was wrong.

All it did was make me see things that weren't there.

I mean, it was surreal, man. Not since my days inhaling cannabis have I had such an out-of-body experience. And the timing couldn't have been worse. I drank the shake, ran out the door, and then took the stage. I was about to address the crowd when the psychedelic effect of the shake hit me—*hard*.

I swear I could see dead people, and I said so.

My team was quick to scrub the transcript of my speech on the website. But, since I've promised to run the most transparent administration in history, here's what I said . . .

"On this Memorial Day, as our nation honors its unbroken line of fallen heroes—**and I see many of them in the audience here today**—our sense of patriotism is particularly strong."

—Me[14]

20

CHAPTER 9

Smarter Than a Fifth Grader?

It's tough being the president of the world—I mean, the country. I'm not complaining, but for the record, I should have known better than to have agreed to be paired with a vice president who hasn't learned how to count to three.

Unlike Joe Biden, I learned basic math and I *do* know how to count.

I can count that there are two years left as president unless my poll numbers reverse their downward spiral—which I blame on the mess George Bush left behind.

I can count that I've played golf thirty-two times in the first sixteen months as president, which happens to be more than George Bush played in eight years.

I can count the number of times I've reached across the ideological aisle by inviting Rush Limbaugh to the White House: zero.

I can count because I'm an educated man. So imagine my surprise when I learned that my running mate during the 2008 election couldn't do something as simple as counting the number of letters in the word "jobs." It's clearly a four-letter word, much like damn, sh*t, f——k, and Bush.

Frankly, I think Joe Biden would lose in the first round of that television show *Are You Smarter Than a Fifth Grader?* Why do I say that? Here's what my veep nominee told Ohio voters during a 2008 election stump speech when he was slamming John McCain . . .

"Look, John's last-minute economic plan does nothing to tackle the number-one job facing the middle class, and it happens to be, as Barack says, a three-letter word: Jobs. J-O-B-S, jobs."

—Joe Biden, criticizing GOP nominee John McCain, October 15, 2008[15]

CHAPTER 10

Pants on Fire

Over the Christmas break of 2009 I was in Hawaii doing a little snorkeling, playing a few rounds of golf, and shooting hoops. I was about to tee off on the ninth hole when my security detail reported there'd been a scuffle on an airplane.

"Sir, there's been another attempted Islamic terrorist attack—"

"Son, you don't work for George Bush. You work for me. In *my* White House we don't identify the nationality in these situations."

"Right, beggin' your pardon."

"Go on. What happened?" I swung my putter while he talked.

"A twenty-three-year-old Nigerian-born Muslim, Abdul Farouk Abdulmutallab—"

"Son, stick to the facts. His name, faith, and country of origin don't matter."

"Uh, okay. A guy boarded Northwest Airlines Flight 253 and tried to light his crotch on fire. Technically he tried to ignite explosives *in* his underpants."

"I see. Wasn't he on the 'no fly' list?" I asked, working on my swing.

"Actually, no. A month ago his father warned the U.S. embassy in Abuja, Nigeria—I mean, in a foreign country that his boy might be, um, a threat."

"How'd we catch him? Air marshal on board? A vigilant TSA agent?"

"No. The passengers tackled him."

"You're saying Homeland Security dropped the ball? Fine. Have Janet Napolitano handle this one while I get back to my game." Leave it to her to say . . .

"The system worked."

—Janet Napolitano, Homeland Security director[16]

CHAPTER 11

As Authentic As I Wanna Be

When I was running for president, my wife reminded me that I can't please all of the people all of the time, but that I would be able to please most of the people most of the time. What Michelle neglected to tell me is that when it comes to the Reverend Jesse Jackson, you can't please him *any* of the time. I'm convinced nothing makes the guy happy—not even my success as the first black man to win the White House.

All I can figure is that Jesse Jackson doesn't think I'm "authentically black."

Look, even though technically I'm half white, I've got as much street cred as Reverend Jackson. I'm every bit as authentic as he is. Maybe he's forgotten those long, lonely years I spent in the wilderness working the community organizer circuit. You know, visiting run-down community centers in Chicago, sitting in uncomfortable plastic chairs, eating greasy food, talking sh*t about The Man while recruiting for ACORN.

And don't forget my lifelong friendship with Reverend Jeremiah Wright—and you don't get more authentic than that guy. He's as hard-core as they come. For twenty years I was a member of his church. I sat in the pew hanging on every word Reverend Jeremiah Wright preached. I even shouted "Amen!" when Reverend Wright said they will "attack you if you try to point out what's going on in *white America*—the U.S. of KKKA."[17] Hell, he was like a father figure to me. He even presided over my marriage to Michelle and baptized my two daughters.

But, because I'm a bigger man than Jesse will ever aspire to be, I want him to know right now that I forgive him for saying . . .

"See, Barack's been talking down to black people . . . I wanna cut his nuts off."

—Jesse Jackson[18]

CHAPTER 12

Killing Birthgate

I need to vent about something for a minute.

I think it's important for me to cover a topic popular with the narrow-minded, birther conspiracy crowd: my original birth certificate.

For the life of me I cannot understand what the big deal is.

I've got several, so pick one already and let's move on.

If you haven't figured it out yet, having several countries of origin is a great way to foster solid international relations. Which is why I have one from Kenya and one from Indonesia. And, for good measure, I've got one from Hawaii, which, it seems, is the most important one for aspiring presidents to have. As an added bonus, I've got both long- and short-form versions just to cover the bases. Copies of these can be found everywhere on the internet. So, to the birthers I say: Go grab 'em and wallpaper your kitchen with 'em. Knock yourselves out.

And while I'm venting, it's a well-established fact that I attended Harvard Law School, where I graduated magna cum laude. Frankly, how I got into Harvard and how I paid my way through that school is none of anyone's damn business. What's more, why should anyone need to see my academic records from Harvard? Or Columbia University? Or my records from Punahou school? Or my passport?

It's true, I did pay a team of lawyers millions to hide my grades, articles, and college thesis from public scrutiny. So what? The simple explanation is that I happen to be concerned about *identity theft*. Why? Because there are just too many people who want to be me.

Now, to those birthers who remain unconvinced, all I can say is . . .

"I can't spend all of my time with my birth certificate plastered on my forehead."

—Me[19]

CHAPTER 13

Stand and Be Counted

I'll state something a little controversial here—but please don't misunderstand me. I love the handicapped. And yet, to be perfectly honest, they're often used by politicians as props. I'm not above leveraging the handicapped for the greater good. It's done all the time.

Pointing to a white guy in the audience who likes my health-care plan, for example, is useless. Put him in a wheelchair and he's golden.

Likewise, make up whatever story you want, the media won't check the facts on a guy if he can't walk or talk or hug his children.

It's a trump card. And it's one that is simply impossible to screw up.

Is the economy bad? Bring out a mentally handicapped girl who works at McDonald's and everyone will forget their troubles. Need to pass a massive environmental bill? Bring out a girl with a missing limb that her mother claims is due to mercury in the water. *Presto!* Want to pass a massive tax increase? Wheel out a single mom of six who was tossed from her job by a wealthy businessman because she never showed up for work on time, and millions will ignore the fact that he is a creator of jobs and has a business to run.

It's so easy, it's almost cheating.

Outside of absolute stupidity, it's just impossible to mess up the powerful emotional effect of a handicapped supporter.

In fact, I believe it's happened only once in the history of politics.

You can probably guess who the moron was who told the physically disabled state senator Chuck Graham to stand

"Chuck, stand up,
let the people see you . . .
Oh, God love ya . . .
What am I talking about?"

—Joe Biden[20]

A Class Act

Believe it or not, running a smart and classy administration means a lot to me. You see, I attended a very snooty college. In fact, two of them: Columbia University and Harvard. Either one qualifies me to look down upon you and the rest of the country. While I was there, I learned to appreciate and use big words. I was taught complex concepts and how to make them even more incomprehensible.

This is why I like to shove through gigantic pieces of legislation numbering thousands of pages. I know that there's no way you could possibly understand what's in 'em, so you'll just have to trust me. For the most part, this strategy has worked quite nicely. The public follows the media's lead as they fawn over me, my illustrious speeches, and my massive command of, uh, English.

One problem. I discovered that I couldn't possibly be expected to fill my staff with people of my caliber. There simply aren't ten or twelve like me in the world.

Still, I tried.

I took a chance on Rahm Emanuel to be my chief of staff. Even though he, like me, attended two universities, Sarah Lawrence (who?) and Northwestern (Big Ten? Give me a break), neither of them will ever be confused with Ivy League schools. Still, since he was once a ballet dancer, I believed he had the stuff to keep my White House classy. In our initial meetings, he used several big words. As amazing as this may seem, I even had to look up a couple in the dictionary.

You can imagine my disappointment when, several months after he joined my team, I learned how Rahm, in a rage, barked at a male member of his staff . . .

"Take your f——king tampon out and tell me what you have to say."

—Rahm Emanuel[21]

CHAPTER 15

Dear Diary

Al Gore's in the headlines with troubling revelations made by several masseuses who claim he sexually assaulted them. These inconvenient truths prompted me to do a word search of him in my diary. I also word-searched "bozo." Don't ask me why.

★

8-4-1974
Dear Diary, For my thirteenth birthday, I watched the movie *Love Story*. I was so moved by the chemistry between that Harvard Law student Oliver Barrett and that hot chick Jennifer Cavilleri. Makes me want to go to Harvard.

★

12-11-1997
Dear Diary, Just found out from Al Gore on CNN that he and Tipper were the real inspiration behind the characters in *Love Story*! I hope I can be like Gore one day. Except I want to be able to talk without sounding as wooden as a lumberjack.

★

6-21-2003

Dear Diary, What the f——k! Al and Tipper were not really the inspiration for *Love Story*. What an embarrassment he has become. I wouldn't even hire him as a community-organizing assistant.

★

1-24-2005

Dear Diary, I'm thinking of running for president. Al Gore is one of the guys I'd really like to get behind me on this in spite of his *Love Story* gaffe. He has a million wackadoodle environmentalists who will do whatever he says.

★

1-16-2008

Dear Diary, Al Gore has said he will do whatever it takes to help me become president of the United States. How can I find a way to tell him to hide? Is it just me or does this guy remind you of a bobblehead?

★

4-18-2010

Dear Diary, One thing I really like about Al Gore is no matter how freaky left-wing I am about the environment, he remains far to the left of me.

★

6-12-2010

Dear Diary, I was talking to a friend recently about the internet and how amazing it all is. And he said, "I remember some bozo politician from Tennessee claiming he invented it." Don't ask me why, but I have a hunch who it might be.

★

That's when I learned . . .

"During my service in the United States Congress, I took the initiative in creating the internet."

—Al Gore[22]

CHAPTER 16

Bare All, Tell All

After winning the 2008 election, my first order of business was to assemble the best possible team. Knowing I needed the brightest players in the field, I put together a comprehensive questionnaire with sixty-three probing questions. All applicants seeking employment on my staff were required to fill it out.

Question 8
Briefly describe the most controversial matters you have been involved with during the course of your career.

Question 14
If you keep or have ever kept a diary that contains anything that could suggest a conflict of interest or be a possible source of embarrassment to you . . . or the president-elect if it were made public, please describe.

Question 61
Have you had any association with any person, group, or business venture that could be used—even unfairly—to impugn or attack your character and qualifications for government service?

When it came to appointing my czars, you can bet I personally studied each questionnaire to ensure there'd be no surprises. That's when I stumbled on one candidate whose background and experience were exactly what I was looking for . . .

"[In jail] I met all these young radical people of color—I mean really radical, communists and anarchists. And it was, like, 'This is what I need to be a part of' . . . I was a rowdy nationalist on April 28, and then the verdicts came down on April 29. By August, I was a communist."

—Van Jones, former green jobs czar[23]

CHAPTER 17

Open Mouth, Insert Foot

March 23, 2010, was to be my date with history.

It was supposed to be the highlight of my political career.

You see, after twisting arms, threatening delegates while they showered, and bribing votes with millions of dollars in pork—in short, utilizing the tools of the political trade I'd learned back in Chicagoland, I had pulled off a legislative triumph unmatched in U.S. history:

The passage of socialized medicine, I mean, ObamaCare.

As I got dressed for the historic signing in the East Room, I remember thinking how proud my Marxist professors would be of my accomplishment. After all, with this single piece of legislation, I was about to place one-sixth of the U.S. economy under the control of the government. I'd done what generations of socialist-leaning Democrats had only dreamed of doing.

And yes, this was to be my day in the sun. Everything was going as planned, that is, until a dark cloud rained on the event. I'm speaking about being upstaged by The Mouth. People often wonder why I need to take so many expensive vacations. The answer is quite simple: Joe Biden.

I should have seen it coming.

I should have known better.

All I asked was for Joe to introduce me to the adoring masses.

Leave it to Joe to say the one thing that grabbed all of the headlines . . .

"Ladies and gentlemen,
the president of the United
States, Barack Obama . . .
This is a big f——king deal."

—Joe Biden, March 23, 2010

CHAPTER 18

Show Me Some Love, Joe

I'm loved all around the world . . . except by Joe Biden.

In Kenya, on the same day I beat John McCain in a landside election victory, more than half of the fifteen babies born in the New Nyanza Provincial Hospital were named after *me* and Michelle—five boys were given my name, Barack Obama, and three girls were named after my wife, Michelle.[24]

How's that for showing me some love?

Then, six short weeks after I was coronated president, children everywhere across America were singing my praises—*literally*. I was delighted to be the subject of their adoration at the B. Bernice Young Elementary School, wherein eighteen very bright eight-year-old students sang songs like, "Mm mm, mm! Barack Hussein Obama / He said red, yellow, black or white / All are equal in his sight," and "Hello, Mr. President we honor you today! / For all your great accomplishments, we all doth say 'Hooray!'"[25]

Amen and Amen!

Did I mention the numerous elementary, middle, and high schools that have been renamed after me? Or the countless honorary doctorates I've received from universities like Notre Dame? Or the love bestowed upon me with a Nobel Peace Prize? After all I've done to this country, uh, *for* this country, you'd think my veep would give me some props, too—that's "praise," for those of you in suburbia.

Which is why I could have wrung his neck when Joe announced . . .

"The single most successful, the single most persuasive, the single most strategic leader I have ever worked with is Nancy Pelosi."

—Joe Biden[26]

CHAPTER 19

Clowns to the Left, Jokers to the Right

*** CONFIDENTIAL ***

MEMO TO: Tim Kaine, Chairman, Democratic National Committee
MEMO BY: President B.O.
MEMO RE: New Recruits

Tim: I'm deeply concerned about the recent flood of incompetent Democratic senators and representatives currently holding office. At the top of the list is Representative Hank Johnson. Where the hell did you dig up this whack job?

Did you hear what he said the other day in that House Armed Services Committee hearing over sending additional troops to Guam? With a straight face, Representative Johnson actually told Admiral Robert Willard, the four-star commander of the Navy's Pacific Fleet: "My fear is that the whole island will become so overly populated that it will tip over and capsize."[27] What the hell?! Was Johnson smoking weed? Doesn't he know Guam is attached to the ocean floor?

It's not a damn raft.

Question: Is there a lack of necessary funds to field qualified candidates? If so, please tell me. I'll find the money. You've got to do better vetting these characters at the local level. And, since you're doing such a piss-poor job of it, let me give you a heads-up. I don't want one dime going to support Alvin Greene, who, as you well know, is a South Carolina Democratic Senate candidate.

Talk about a doozy, Greene said . . .

"Another thing we can do for jobs is make toys of me, especially for the holidays. Little dolls. Me. Like maybe little action dolls. Me in an army uniform, air force uniform, and me in my suit. They can make toys of me and my vehicle, especially for the holidays and Christmas for the kids. That's something that would create jobs. So you see I think out of the box like that. It's not something a typical person would bring up. That's something that could happen, that makes sense. It's not a joke."

—Alvin Greene, Democratic Senate candidate[28]

CHAPTER 20

Joey's Disease

I went to get my annual physical the other day, the results of which won't be released to the general public. Before Sean Hannity gets on my case about that, let me ask you something: Would *you* want the world to have access to *your* personal medical records? I better clarify my question because, thanks to the recently passed ObamaCare bill with its mandatory shared medical database provision, we in the government already know your private data.

What I'm asking is whether you would want the *National Enquirer* or *People* magazine to report how much you weigh . . . your blood pressure and cholesterol levels . . . and whether there are trace amounts of, uh, drugs in your system?

I didn't think so.

Neither do I.

This much I will reveal. I asked my doc if it were medically possible for me to catch whatever Joe has that causes him to screw up so many times when talking to the press. When my doc asked why I thought I might be catching Joey's gaffing disease, I told him about the time a tornado hit a town in Kansas. It was a terrible thing. The photos were chilling. Entire city blocks were swept away in the powerful winds. Tragically, twelve people died.

When the press caught up with me and asked for a comment, I'm embarrassed to say I pulled a Biden. I mangled the facts beyond belief . . .

"In case you missed it this week, there was a tragedy in Kansas. Ten thousand people died—an entire town destroyed."

—Me[29]

CHAPTER 21

What the F——K?

Most Americans have suspicions about my economic plan—spend until there's no more money, then spend way more money, then spend, spend, spend. Then there are no jobs and Big Government becomes momma.

And they need momma to survive.

Simply put: Spending equals power.

Now, I explained this formula of controlling the people to Joey. With a flash of his pearly white teeth, he gave me that goofy smile that said, "I don't understand a word you said."

Most of the time, I hate that. But when it comes to the economy, I love it.

See, Joe Biden also has a form of Tourette's. Instead of a jerky motion or spitting out cuss words, Joe coughs up whatever is on his mind—no matter how senseless, illogical, or revealing.

So when the national media asked him to explain my economic plan, I was quite concerned. If he were to have told them what I told him in private, there would have been hell to pay.

Ah, but that's where Joe's disease became a gift from heaven above.

What he said was so nonsensical—such a goofy version of what I explained to him behind closed doors—that everybody in the press just froze like deer in the headlights. I could tell they were as confused as all get out. In fact, they became as confused as he was . . . which is why they dropped the story after Joe said . . .

"People, when I say that, look at me and say, 'What are you talking about, Joe? You're telling me we have to go spend money to keep from going bankrupt?' The answer is yes."

—Joe Biden[30]

CHAPTER 22

How Dumb Are They in Nevada?

That's what I ask myself every time I watch Senate majority leader Harry Reid dig himself out of a pickle. I like Harry, in spite of the fact that he once called me a "light-skinned" African-American "with no Negro dialect"[31]—unless I wanted to have one. Look, the guy is a useful idiot, okay? Besides, he's apologized already.

No harm, no foul.

The truth is, I can only hope that I'll be able to sling the bullsh*t as well as he does when I get to be his age.

Case in point.

It's a well-known fact that Harry's home state of Nevada had something like a 4.4 percent unemployment rate when he became the leader of the Senate. By the fall of 2010, unemployment for Nevadans skyrocketed to 14.3 percent, which ranks up there among the highest in the nation. I'm sure I didn't help their sagging economy when I said Americans shouldn't blow a bunch of cash on Vegas when they're trying to save for college. Let's set that aside.

The larger issue is that *Harry* was the one who pushed through my economic porkulus, I mean, stimulus packages, TARP, the nationalizing of GM, and ObamaCare in the Senate. The fact that those spending initiatives and power grabs failed to reverse what George Bush did to the country would have hamstrung the average politician. Not Harry. With a straight face—can the guy even smile?—he told the most boldfaced lie I've heard in recent times. And it's just possible the voters in Nevada will gamble their future on a guy who had the balls to say . . .

"You know that I had nothing to do with the massive foreclosures here. You know that I had nothing to do with these unemployment figures."

—Harry Reid, Democratic Senate majority leader[32]

CHAPTER 23

The New Dog in Town

There's a cynical piece of advice in Washington, D.C., that folks usually tell the newbies who move into town: "If you want a friend in Washington, get a dog." I, of course, don't have that problem. I've got plenty of friends.

And I can always buy more if I need 'em.

However, I did make a campaign promise to Malia and Sasha that I'd get them a dog once we got here. As you know, I've fulfilled that promise with the gift of Bo. The girls couldn't be happier with their baby Portuguese water dog, which, like me, is a black and white mix. While the girls are thrilled with this rambunctious puppy, there's one person who hates little Bo-Bama: Rahm Emanuel.

Three reasons come to mind why my former chief of staff despised our pet.

First, I think Rahm finally had met his match. The fact of the matter is that Bo snarled every time Rahm came around the family quarters as if he were the Son of the Devil's Spawn. Bo's smart. He's a good judge of character. I'd say he had every reason to growl at the sight of Rahm.

Second, Rahm hated cleaning up after Bo when he tinkled in the Oval Office—especially after I put in that new rug.

Third, I kept Rahm on a tighter leash than Bo. If there's one thing Rahm couldn't stand, it was the fact that he wasn't the top dog anymore. That's the real reason he left the White House. And, just to be clear about one thing, Rahm, I know what you said regarding Bo . . .

"I'm going to kill that f——king dog."

—Rahm Emanuel, former chief of staff[33]

CHAPTER 24

Never Admit You Suck

While searching for the right running mate in 2008, I had this text conversation on my BlackBerry with my vetting committee.

Me: Hey, VP vetting committee: Why not Hillary?

VetCom: Two words: Bill Clinton.

Me: She's smart. Knows what's up. Can think on her feet.

VetCom: Exactly.

Me: Elaborate.

VetCom: Dude, the smarter your VP is, the dumber you look. You want a real boob. Some ignoramus who makes you look smarter than God.

Me: Quayleish?

VetCom: He's closet smart. Think flat-out *dumb*. We have a lot to choose from at DNC. Resumes are to the roof. Howard Dean, Harry Reid, Barbara Boxer. The list is busting at the seams.

Me: Conyers?

VetCom: LOL. We said "dumb," not "throws up on himself." Think more along the lines of Joe Biden.

Me: LMAO.

VetCom: Seriously.

Me: Biden? Guys, Biden is an embarrassment. If we could wire his jaw shut, then fine.

VetCom: Look, he's perfect. Dumb, but too dumb to know it. That's exactly what you want. If he were any smarter, he'd realize how dumb he was and then he'd blow the whole charade.

Me: What if you're wrong?

VetCom: We're confident he won't disappoint you, sir.

"Hillary Clinton is as qualified or more qualified than I am to be vice president of the United States of America. Quite frankly, it might have been a better pick than me. She's qualified to be president. I mean that sincerely, she's first-rate."

—Joe Biden[34]

CHAPTER 25

Suddenly, Imus Looks Like a Diplomat

My grandmother—may she rest in peace—was a typical white person.

Now, I don't hold that against her. She was born that way. The fact of the matter is in spite of her ethnicity, she gave me some of the best advice I'd ever received in my life . . . She'd say things like, "Barry, always be sure to *think* first before you say anything." This explains why I, uh, why I say "uh" so much, because I'm, uh, thinking before, you know, speaking.

She also told me, "If you have nothing good to say, don't say anything at all."

I can't say that I've always followed that bit of advice.

Take, for example, my appearance on the *Tonight Show* with Jay Leno. Frankly, it felt good to have the eyes of the world on me as we talked about my favorite topic: me. Frankly, Jay had a way of making me feel relaxed—unlike that Pastor Rick Warren who had the nerve to ask me heavy questions about when life begins in the womb, you know, stuff that's way above my pay grade.

So, there I was trading laughs and talking about my first couple of months as president, when Leno asked me about the White House bowling alley. It's no secret that I'm about as good at bowling as Dan Quayle was at spelling. I wasn't about to sugarcoat that fact, so I blurted out a little self-deprecating joke.

The moment I said those words, I just knew Sarah Palin was gonna have my ass over it. But I think we all need to come together and realize it wasn't like I called someone a "nappy-headed ho." All I said was . . .

"I bowled a 129 . . . It was like Special Olympics or something."

—Me[35]

CHAPTER 26

Not in My Bed

This might surprise you, but not all of Joe Biden's gaffes bother me.

Some have actually helped my run for the highest office in the land.

For example, I was thrilled when Joe, talking about me, said, "You got the first mainstream African-American who is articulate and bright and clean and a nice-looking guy. I mean, that's a storybook, man."[36]

As you might expect, the press, thinking Joe had hurled a personal insult, was quick to pick up and run with his remark. What's more, talk radio and the late-night comedy shows had a field day with the fact that Biden said I was "clean." Literally overnight I was positioned in the public's eye as a clean, attractive candidate.

There are two reasons why I wasn't offended. First, he was historically inaccurate. There were other African-American presidential candidates who ran for office before me—Jesse Jackson, Shirley Chisholm, Carol Moseley Braun, and Al Sharpton come to mind. I'd say all of them were articulate, bright, clean, and nice-looking—maybe with the exception of Al Sharpton on a bad hair day.

The other reason why I wasn't bothered by the remark is a bit personal.

You see, I have a dirty little secret.

Leave it to my wife to open her mouth and spill the beans. Michelle is just like that. I'm amazed that someone as bright as she is would broadcast to the world our dirty laundry. Fortunately, Joe's comment that I'm "clean" gave me cover when Michelle blabbed this little detail about our children . . .

"We have this ritual in the morning. They come in my bed [only] if Dad isn't there—because he's too snore-y and stinky, they don't want to ever get into bed with him."

—Michelle Obama[37]

CHAPTER 27

Naked as a Jaybird

Before I came to Washington I had this mental picture of how laws were enacted in the nation's capital. It was an expectation shaped primarily by those pictures of our Founding Fathers featured in my history books. I remember studying prominent statesmen like Benjamin Franklin, John Adams, and Thomas Jefferson, men who liked to wax eloquent while engaging in spirited discussions about independence and such.

In other words, they engaged in civil discourse.

I assumed that the grand tradition of reasonable men and women exercising a certain degree of decorum while debating the issues of the day would be the norm. I was wrong. As president, I've been able to pull back the political veil and really see how things get done in D.C. . . . and it's a lot closer to how we did things in Chicago.

You might say it's more of a balls-to-the-wall ordeal.

For example, if I want to get something done, like the passage of the stimulus bill, health care, cap-and-trade, or whatever, I just pick up the phone and call my former chief enforcer, Rahm Emanuel. Rahm had a way of whipping the troops back into line like nobody I had ever worked with before.

Anytime, anywhere, Rahm would hunt down wayward congressmen—even in the shower if necessary—and read them the riot act. While I can't picture old Ben Franklin pulling a stunt like that, I say "whatever works."

Put it this way. Rahm had a reputation as someone who would sell his mother to get a vote. He didn't easily throw in the towel, as Eric Massa can attest . . .

"I am showering, naked as a jaybird, and here comes Rahm Emanuel, not even with a towel wrapped round his tush, poking his finger in my chest, yelling at me because I wasn't going to vote for the president's budget. Do you know how awkward it is to have a political argument with a naked man?"

—Eric Massa, ex–Democratic congressman[38]

CHAPTER 28

Out of the Mouths of Babes

The other day, I sat down in my daughters' room to have a little bed-time chat. I usually have one of my staff members do that, but I was feeling all warm and fuzzy inside so I thought I'd do it myself. Sasha asked me a childlike but brilliant question.

"Daddy, is truth always truth?"

A tough question to answer. I mean, truth is how you define it, right? I told her what any father would say: "Honey, that depends on three things—to *whom* you're talking, *when* you're talking to them, and *what* you want out of them."

She smiled and nodded, clearly understanding the nuances.

Then Malia chimed in with a question of her own.

"Daddy, is right always right?"

I stood up, took a deep breath, and made sure I had their attention. "Kids. If it's right, it's right. You can't be right and wrong at the same time. It's simple logic."

Sasha chimed back in. "That's what we thought. So, if you do the right thing all the time, you'll always be right."

"Of course, dear," I explained. "Only an idiot doesn't understand that."

"Okay but—" Malia hesitated. "That Mr. Biden guy you sent to talk to us last night, he told us something completely different."

Sasha cut in quickly. "Yeah, we tried to explain that if you're right, you're right, but he just didn't get it. Do you know what he told us, Dad?"

"If we do everything right, if we do it with absolute certainty, there's still a 30 percent chance we're going to get it wrong."

—Joe Biden[39]

CHAPTER 29

One Flu over the Cuckoo's Nest

As I type this, I'm flying in Air Force One on my way to Camp David for a little well-earned R&R after delivering my N1H1 swine flu speech. I love making these speeches. It's crisis time, man! Which means it's time to leverage the public fear and sell them another reason to be glad *I'm* in charge.

It's like something my former chief of staff, Rahm Emanuel, once said: "You never want a serious crisis to go to waste."[40] Which is why I love standing before my nation telling them to remain calm. There's nothing more exhilarating than that. You know, assuring the peeps I have it under control. I'm your daddy.

Look, I know the people are sheep. They naturally panic. That's when leaders lead. Oh, and it's so easy, too. The script has been prewritten since the dawn of time. All I have to do is smile and say, "Stay calm. There's nothing to fear. See? I'm still flying. Go about your business as usual." The public swoons. Mr. President says it's okay, so it must be okay. What's more, the business community likes it when I comfort the crowds, because panicky people don't go out and travel and spend money. The economy suffers. We all know I can't afford more bad economic news.

And, yes, thanks to me, the panic will die down because panics are just that—panics. When things return to normal, the folks will all say, "Obama is so smart. How did he know?"

Hang on, I'm getting a text from my press secretary . . . It's a "What do to" question. Ah, sh*t. Joe's done it again. He just told the American people the exact opposite thing of my message . . .

"I would tell members of my family—and I have— I wouldn't go anywhere in confined places right now. It's not that it's going to Mexico, it's that you are in a confined aircraft when one person sneezes, it goes everywhere through the aircraft. That's me."

—Joe Biden[41]

CHAPTER 30

I Had a Dream

People sometimes ask me when I first thought about becoming the president of the United States. In short, the seeds of that idea took root when I was a student attending Occidental College. Since I came from poverty and, frankly, had no place to live, I worked the system. I found and sponged off a very wealthy student from Pakistan, Mohammed Hasan Chandoo. Using my skills as a smooth talker, I endeared myself to Chandoo. We quickly became roommates.

That was my break. Chandoo lived in one of the biggest and nicest houses in town. He threw lavish parties and spread money around as if he had a direct pipeline from the Middle East—which he probably did. Best of all, we rode everywhere in his late-model BMW. We'd go out to dinner and he'd pick up the tab. We'd smoke and drink the night away, and kick around the merits of Marxism.

To be honest, I thought, "I could get used to this." You know, living high on the hog at someone else's expense. One problem. At first I couldn't think of an occupation where I could maintain that lifestyle, until one of my drinking buddies quipped, "Barry, why not become the president? He has free room and board. He gets to throw big parties without worrying about the tab. There's plenty of interns if he wants them. And, there's lot's of free golf."

Right then and there I knew what I had to do. I had to be president.

When I moved to Chicago, I hooked up with the folks who could steer my career in the right direction. One of them was my good friend Professor Bill Ayers. He seemed like my kind of guy, even though he's said a few crazy things . . .

"Kill all the rich people. Break up their cars and apartments. Bring the revolution home. Kill your parents."

—Bill Ayers[42]

CHAPTER 31

Fair and Balanced?

Nancy Pelosi is like Stalin in a Skirt.

Maybe Mussolini in Makeup.

Say what you want about her, but you got to admit that girl has balls. She'll do *whatever* it takes to get her, uh, I mean my pet projects passed. Nothing stops her—not her unfavorable poll numbers, her lack of a grasp on the issues, or the will of the majority of the American people, who think she's off her rocker.

Nancy'll swing that gavel like she's Rambo ready to clobber the opposition.

That said, the other day Glenn Beck and those mean-spirited journalists on the network that rhymes with "Botox" really crossed a line. They blasted Madam Pelosi for her comment about the need to quickly pass my health-care bill. They certainly weren't "fair and balanced" on that one.

Look, these are the facts. It's true, Pelosi *did* say: "We have to pass the bill so that you can find out what is in it."[43]

What's the big deal with that?

I remember when I was a kid suffering from constipation, my grandmother would say, "Barry, you'll have to pass a stool so we can all find out what's in it." Hell, that's the same sort of thing doctors say all the time. You know, "Myrtle, you'll have to pass a kidney stone so we can see what's in it." Makes perfect sense to me. I ask you: Did the Fox network interview any gastrointestinal specialists to defend the idea that sometimes you must pass something before you really know what's in it? Nope. I rest my case.

Now, what didn't make sense to me is when Nancy Pelosi said . . .

"Bipartisanship is a two-way street. But let me say this. The bill can be bipartisan, even though the votes might not be bipartisan, because they [Republicans] have made their imprint on this."

—Nancy Pelosi[44]

CHAPTER 32

The Oral Office

Sometimes late at night I like to be alone in the Oval Office just sipping a Coke through a crazy straw one of my girls gave me as a gift. Sitting there with my feet up on the desk, I can't help but look around the room and imagine the rich history made in that very room. One by one those great predecessors left their mark on history within these hallowed walls. Why, in my lifetime alone . . .

John F. Kennedy addressed Americans on the Soviet arms buildup in Cuba.

Richard Nixon announced his resignation.

Gerald Ford pardoned Richard Nixon.

Jimmy Carter, well, not much to talk about there.

Ronald Reagan comforted the nation after the *Challenger* disaster.

George H. W. Bush announced we were going to war in the Persian Gulf.

Bill Clinton . . .

Damn. He and Monica Lewinsky really did the wild thang in the Oval Office. I thought, "Bill, you must have been thinking with the wrong head, brother." I mean, how could *anybody* take the man seriously after pulling that stunt? He'll be forever remembered as the guy who single-handedly made millions of Americans debate whether oral sex was really having sex.

I decided right then and there that I didn't want to make the same mistake. I knew the wise thing for me to do was to speak to the other presidents and ask for their advice. Which I did, but I managed to insult Nancy Reagan in the process . . .

"In terms of speaking to former presidents, I've spoken to all of them that are living . . . I didn't want to get into a Nancy Reagan thing about, you know, doing any séances."

—Me[45]

CHAPTER 33

Long Live King Obama

Let's review a few definitions from *Webster's Dictionary*:

President: an elected official serving as both chief of state and chief political executive in a republic having a presidential government.

King: a male monarch of a major territorial unit; especially: one whose position is hereditary and who rules for life.

The distinction is monumental. The United States government specifically notes that difference. It was in his Gettysburg Address that Abraham Lincoln reminded a weary nation that we have a "government of the people, by the people, for the people." Kings, on the contrary, simply rule.

Mind you, I kind of like that idea. "King Obama" sounds so much better than President Obama. I mean, a company president can be tossed by board members who don't like the direction of a company. THE president can be tossed out on his ass by voters who don't like the direction of a country.

But you can't touch a king without blood on your hands. Kings can decree anything they please—and the masses will bow and shout, "Long live the king!" I get goose bumps just thinking about it. No Congress to coddle. No voters to fear. And—*bonus!*—you own the courts. Alas, I am but a president.

Only my closest confidants know my true desires.

But when I hired our friend Valerie Jarrett to be my senior advisor and assistant for public engagement and intergovernmental affairs, I didn't think I'd have to remind her to keep her fat mouth shut . . .

"[George Bush] will be the president until January 20th. However, giving— given, really, the daunting challenges that we face, it's important that President-elect Obama is prepared to really take power and begin to **rule** Day One."

—Valerie Jarrett[46]

CHAPTER 34

Off the Reservation

I'm the first African-American to become president—that's assuming you don't count Bill Clinton, who was called, by Nobel Prize winner Toni Morrison, "blacker than any actual black person who could ever be elected in our children's lifetime." What is clear is that I pulled in unimaginable numbers of minority voters.

According to CNN, I had 67 percent of Latino voters, 63 percent of Asian voters, and an astounding 96 percent of black voters. And, thanks to ACORN, 100 percent of the dead voters. I realize those are a lot of numbers to deal with. So I'll put this in terms that even Joe Biden should be able to understand: I kicked serious booty.

Minorities understand that Barack Obama is one of them. He's a man who will leave no minority behind.

I just wish I'd left that white guy behind.

If I could—and it turns out I can—I'd fire every bonehead involved with the abysmal vetting of Jokin' Joe Biden.

There I was, about to become the first African-American president in U.S. history. I walked into a convenience store to shake hands and kiss babies and pretend I was one of the regular guys before hopping back into my armored limousine and immersing myself in hand sanitizer. The press was eating it up.

But the moment was ruined for me when some punk reminded me of Biden's remark a few years earlier. What should have been a celebration of the growth of the Indian-American population in Delaware was turned into a cheap stereotype you'd expect from a white guy living in a mobile home, all because Joe had said . . .

"You cannot go into a 7-11 or a Dunkin' Donuts unless you have a slight Indian accent. Oh, I'm not joking."

—Joe Biden[47]

CHAPTER 35

Sour Grapes

I attended Punahou School in Hawaii, which is one of the most elite private institutions of learning in the country. Think "the Ritz Carlton of schools," if that helps. In spite of the school's crème de la crème reputation, I quickly learned that boys will be boys—and these boys engaged in frequent pissing contests back behind the building during recess.

I, for one, didn't participate. Never saw the point.

Plus, I was afraid I might not be able to zip things up and, uh, close the barn doors, as it were. You see, my mom was a single parent back then and all we could afford were secondhand jeans with defective zippers. I didn't want to walk around after recess with my johnson exposed.

Years later when I entered politics, I discovered that grown men still engaged in pissing contests. Take my former governor Rod Blagojevich. For unknown reasons, Rod tried to draw me into a pissing contest the other day, saying, "I'm blacker than Barack Obama. I shined shoes. I grew up in a five-room apartment. My father had a little Laundromat in a black community not far from where we lived. I saw it all growing up."[48]

I refused to take the bait except to say, yo, Rod, guess what? I'm not that pencil-thin, wet-behind-the-ears junior senator from Illinois anymore. I control the FBI. So shut your big f——king trap.

Like I said, I'm not gonna take the bait. In fact, Rod, I'll tell the FBI to back off if you stop talking trash like this about me . . . Deal?

"It's such a cynical business, and most of the people in the business are full of sh*t and phonies, but I was real, man—and am real. This guy, he was catapulted in on hope and change, what we hope the guy is. What the f——k? Everything he's saying's on the teleprompter."

—Rod Blagojevich[49]

CHAPTER 36

What the Hell Was He Thinking?

Everyone knows I had about a five-second political career in the United States Senate before I ran for the highest office in the land. I had much to prove and little time to prove it. My team recommended that I pick a vice president who could balance what I lacked—things like governing experience, knowledge of foreign policy, legislative initiatives, a genuine U.S. birth certificate. Stuff like that. Anyway, we settled on Joe Biden because he had those things.

Candidly, I had many a sleepless night after picking Joe.

I remember we were about ten weeks from the November 2008 election. I was working overtime distancing myself from a string of nightmares that could have easily torpedoed my candidacy . . . my relationship with the bizarre rants of Reverend Wright, the revelations about what's really going on with ACORN, and questions surrounding my middle name.

I just didn't need any more controversial press.

While I was busy putting out fires, Joe was clearing some brush on his property as the press hovered nearby. He loaded up his pickup truck with logs and rumbled away to dispose of them. When he returned, he said something on camera that, taken out of context, would have been incredibly embarrassing for the ticket.

For the life of me I couldn't figure out why he'd say a thing like this. I figured a guy with four decades in politics would know that everything you say is fodder for the other side to use against you. Frankly, with all of the bathroom humor possibilities of his remark, I'm surprised his sound bite wasn't instantly turned into a ring tone . . .

"I had a successful dump."

—Joe Biden[50]

My ~~Muslim~~ Christian Faith

When it comes to my critics, the elevator doesn't always go to the top floor. There are those who try to make the case that I'm a crypto-Muslim, even though I've publicly stated I'm a Christian. I don't deny they've been effective now that one in five Americans think I'm a Muslim—*Allah be praised.*

The crazies on the right are quick to cite something I said in confidence to Egyptian foreign minister Ahmed Aboul Gheit, namely, "The American president told me in confidence that he is a Muslim."[51] (I've subsequently told him in confidence that he will not be invited to the next Ramadan celebration at the White House.) Since nobody else heard me, that one doesn't count. Which is why they've built their case entirely on conjecture. For example, they point out that I have:

- Declared the "war on terror" is officially over.
- Banned the term "Islamic extremism" from government statements.
- Stated that America is *not* a Christian nation.
- Described America as one of the largest Muslim countries on the planet.
- Ordered NASA to work with more Muslim countries.
- Endorsed the building of a mosque at Ground Zero.

Look, while this partial list of my actions appears damning, as a lawyer I maintain it's nothing more than *circumstantial evidence.* It would be an entirely different matter if I had said that I was a Muslim. Oh, wait, I guess I did . . .

"Let's not play games, what I was suggesting—you're absolutely right that John McCain has not talked about my Muslim faith . . ."

—Me[52]

CHAPTER 38

Magic Talk

I taught at the University of Chicago for a number of years. Of course, there are no records of my class syllabuses and none of the students remember me. No big deal. People have short memories. I can tell you this much. I taught a module on the art of political logic. In short, the goal is to *connect two things that really aren't related but that sound like they are.*

I'd tell my students, "Listen up. As a Democrat you must understand the art of political logic, also known as Magic Talk. This is your secret weapon."

They'd inch forward on their seats awaiting my priceless pearls of insight.

"Here's how it works. If a reporter asks you how you, as president, could possibly binge on Wagyu steak at one hundred dollars a pound and golf while 18 million Americans have lost their jobs, you simply point out that there would have been 25 million Americans out of work if not for your miraculous efforts to save the economy. *Bingo!* You're a hero—plus, you get to keep eating steak and playing golf."

I could see they were getting it.

"Or, if Rush Limbaugh were to point out an apparent contradiction in your position—like claiming to be in favor of traditional marriage while being against any legislation that supports traditional marriage, no worries. Use your Magic Talk."

It even works when someone attacks you over what seems like a violation of the Constitution. Although Representative Phil Hare wasn't one of my students, I'd give him an A+ for his brilliant application of "Magic Talk" when he said . . .

"I don't worry about the Constitution on this . . .
What I care more about,
I care more about the people dying every day who don't have health care."

—Rep. Phil Hare (D-Ill.)[53]

CHAPTER 39

Whistling Dixie

Every once in a while, you meet some boob who absolutely doesn't get it.

You know the guy—a complete nutcase who is guzzling Everclear while the rest of the room is sipping wine.

During my presidential run, one of those guys surfaced—bubbling to the top of the heap like some smelly gas that would be better off left buried far beneath the crust of the earth forever.

This dope bragged about the one thing that is universally considered embarrassing: slavery. Might as well have been telling a group of African-Americans that you're in favor of segregation. But this was a step worse.

In the middle of a discussion about which states would help deliver the South to me during my presidential run, it was pointed out that this particular character lived in a state that wasn't actually part of the South.

What would you do, had you been on my staff?

A. Concede the point.
B. Note that your state shares some of the positive attributes of the Southern states.
C. Insult your state and every Southern state by pointing out that your state is just as guilty of one of society's worst atrocities as those in the South.

Joe Biden chose C.

"You don't know my state.
My state was a slave state.
My state is a border state."

—Joe Biden[54]

CHAPTER 40

Banning Bimbos

Trust me on this. I might be the most powerful man in the world, but I know my limits. There's no way I'd ever fool around on Michelle—even once. If I ever cheated on my wife, unlike Hillary, Michelle wouldn't hesitate to pull a Lorena Bobbitt on me and hack off my, uh, private parts.

Case in point:

In the spring of 2010 we were in the heat of the health-care debate. As you might expect, I was putting in extra-long hours coaching Nancy Pelosi. We were often alone in the Oval Office. Thanks to Bill Clinton, this tends to raise flags with my wife. I remember going to the kitchen to make a snack late one night when I bumped into an angry Michelle—sharpening the knives. I could tell she was pissed by the way she was looking at my zipper.

I said, "Hey, honey. What's up?"

She said, "You were with Nancy an awfully long time tonight—"

"Babe, trust me, we were just working—"

"Working it? That better not be Mr. Happy on the rise."

"*Pleeease,* Michelle. With Nancy? Get real."

"I know how that bitch is," Michelle said, studying the edge of the knife. "That woman gets an idea in her brain—no matter how ridiculous—and she's like Glenn Close in *Fatal Attraction.*"

She's got a point. I'll have to be extra careful, 'cause Pelosi isn't the kind of broad that takes "No" for an answer . . .

"We will go through the gate. If the gate is closed, we will go over the fence. If the fence is too high, we will pole-vault in. If that doesn't work, we will parachute in. But we are going to get health-care reform passed for the American people for their own personal health and economic security and for the important role that it will play in reducing the deficit."

—Nancy Pelosi[55]

CHAPTER 41

Going to Pot

Reporter Chris Matthews dug up an old video clip in which I acknowledged my affinity for smoking pot when I was a youngster. In the video I'm pictured saying, "When I was a kid, I inhaled, frequently. That was the point." I don't deny it. I said it. I'm not gonna pull a Bill Clinton and claim I didn't inhale. *Right*.

Who's gonna believe that sh*t?

Now, the moment Chris aired the video footage, my advisors went crazy. They told me I should sue him for defamation of character. To be honest, I don't hold it against Chris. How could I? I mean, Chris is the kind of reporter you like to keep around. The guy actually gets thrills up his leg whenever he hears me speak.

But I'm starting to think Nancy Reagan was on to something with her "Just Say No" antidrug campaign. Why? I hate to admit this, but there are times when, uh, my memory isn't what it used to be. I forget where I am and what I'm supposed to say. What's worse is that sometimes I'll say the *opposite* of what I intended to say.

Like the time when I took the stage to announce my choice for the vice president slot. I still can't believe I said: "So let me introduce to you the next president, uh, the next *vice* president of the United States of America, Joe Biden."[56]

I attribute that moment to my pot smoking. How else do you explain it?

There's another side effect to heavy cannabis usage.

At times, it acts like a truth serum. Damn if I don't find myself saying what I *really* believe instead of a carefully scripted lie designed to mislead the people . . .

"The reforms we seek would bring greater competition, choice, savings, and **inefficiencies** to our health-care system."

—Me[57]

CHAPTER 42

You Say It's Your Birthday

It's clear to me that white people do birthdays differently from black folks.

Correction: *Some* white people have a rather odd way of celebrating.

Let me illustrate using my forty-ninth birthday.

As you may know, Michelle, who loves to travel the world on the taxpayers' dime, was vacationing in Spain with our daughter Sasha, while Malia was away at summer camp. That left me free to just hang out with a few friends in Chicago for a quiet meal and some cake. There were no shenanigans. No loud music.

I was just chillin' at the old crib in Hyde Park.

Now, it's true that the following day one of my billionaire supporters, Neil Bluhm, threw a birthday party in my honor. Who was I to stop him from leveraging the occasion to raise funds for the DNC? After all, he charged $30,400 a ticket. (I'd say it's worth at least that much to see me.) Now, before you get mad at the price tag, there *was* an option for those on a budget. Another fundraiser/birthday party was arranged across town on the other side of the tracks with tickets going for just $250 a pop.

My point is that for my special day I had the cake, the cards, the presents, and that was about it. Contrast that with how my fellow Democrat Eric Massa, who happens to be white, decided to celebrate his fiftieth birthday. While I wasn't invited and wouldn't have gone even if I had been, this brother had a rather unorthodox way of getting down . . .

"Now, they're saying I groped a male staffer. Yes, I did. Not only did I grope him, I tickled him until he couldn't breathe and four guys jumped on top of me. It was my fiftieth birthday."

—Former Rep. Eric Massa (D-N.Y.)[58]

CHAPTER 43

She Ain't Dead Yet

Relationships with foreign leaders can make or break a presidency. Which explains why I spent so much time bowing down to King Abdullah of Saudi Arabia, Japanese emperor Akihito, and the communist Chinese president Hu Jintao. Hell, I even bow down to the Burger King when I take the kids out for fast food behind Michelle's back. The point is that with each and every leader, there are protocols.

I learned early on that, when greeting one of the wives of a Middle Eastern leader, you must *not* lift up her niqab to give her a friendly peck on the cheek, no matter how tempting. If Bill Clinton—who probably learned that lesson the hard way—hadn't briefed me on that custom, we might be at war with Saudi Arabia right now. For this reason, I surrounded myself with what I *thought* were the best and the brightest, an administration that understood the importance of not just hosting our allies with grace and class but treating them like royalty.

I mean, that's their job. It means a lot when you can congratulate them on the recent arranged marriage of their daughter. Or express the sadness you felt upon hearing of the death of their beloved camel.

But then came the meeting with Ireland's prime minister, Brian Cowen.

Even I could not rescue the world from this moment. Joe Biden, one heartbeat from the presidency, mind you, gave Cowen an introduction that set international relations back two hundred years when he said . . .

"His mom lived in Long Island for ten years or so. God rest her soul. And— although she's, wait, your mom's still—your mom's still alive? Your dad passed. God bless her soul."

—Joe Biden[59]

CHAPTER 44

Back Off, Glenn

I'd like to know where Glenn Beck—that pink-faced, halfwit, former DJ with a measly high-school diploma—keeps getting his information on my choice of czars. I'm beginning to think there's a mole on my staff feeding him the goods. I mean, I busted my ass getting Ron Bloom on board as my manufacturing czar. I even did an end run around the Congress and just appointed him to office.

Two or three days later, Glenn Beck comes out with this obscure videotape of Rod saying, "We know that the free market is nonsense. We know that the whole point is to game the system. We kinda agree with Mao Zedong that power comes largely from the barrel of a gun."[60] Nice, Glenn. Scare the people into thinking my administration is suddenly gonna use guns to control the people.

Hell, I've never even owned a Daisy BB gun.

The same thing happened when I appointed John Holdren to be my science czar, and a couple of days later there's Glenn exposing one of John's socialist sentiments on his damn TV show: "Redistribution of wealth both within and among nations is absolutely essential."[61] What's it to you, Glenn? It's not like he's talking about taking your money and giving it to people who don't want to work.

Uh, that didn't come out quite right.

Anyway, what really fries my bacon—and I do love bacon—was when Glenn started getting personal by going after my dear friend Bill Ayers. Look, I don't attack your friends, so stop going after mine, even if Bill did say . . .

"I don't regret setting bombs. I feel we didn't do enough."

—Bill Ayers[62]

Food Fight

I'm sitting in a school cafeteria as I type this. I just finished speaking in an assembly at Malia and Sasha's school and figured I'd grab a quick lunch with them as soon as they get here. Don't worry, even though it's lunchtime the Secret Service has cleared out the whole room for us. In fact, my security detail will beat the crap out of anybody who tries to enter. Even if it's a kid trying to get his lunch.

In fact, I'm watching a hungry, snot-nosed punk get roughed up right now.

Honestly, I love to watch my guys work. Usually, they take the guy in the back room and give him what-for. But I generally request they do this where I can see them in action. It's sorta like watching a reality TV show in the making. Sometimes I'll get a bag of popcorn and watch 'em nail the intruder.

Right now the little kid is swearing up a storm . . . he's talkin' sh*t like: "F——k you," and, "Give me a f——king break, pal." Such profanity. Such rage. What's gotten into kids these days? What's with the short temper? Can't the kid wait one lousy hour for his lunch?

You know, I've tried to make a point of teaching these children to be patient and respectful, but it's just so difficult for the message to sink in.

What's this? The boy getting roughed up just shouted, "Look, man, I just said the same thing I heard from Joe Biden. You gonna beat him up, too?" Good point.

Memo to self: Tell Joe to tone it down . . . the kids are watching.

"An hour late, oh give me a f——king break."

—Joe Biden[63]

CHAPTER 46

Not You, Too, Nancy

I've been consulting privately with my legal team about my options to remove Joe Biden from his role as vice president. The guy is such a counterproductive embarrassment. Take this cringe-inducing blunder. I think Joe was trying to deflect public criticism of my policies by pointing to the Bush administration. Normally that's a good strategy IF you get your facts straight.

Joe stated that Cheney *"doesn't realize that Article I of the Constitution defines the role of the vice president of the United States, that's the executive—he works in the executive branch. He should understand that. Everyone should understand that."*[64] Wrong-o, again-o, Joe.

The Constitution defines the role of the *legislative* branch.

Sheesh! Even I knew that one.

Now, it's one thing for Joe to pulverize the facts more thoroughly than a Cuisinart on maximum spin. It's another thing for him to rub off on my staff. It seems that others in my administration now think it's okay to misrepresent the facts and stretch the truth because Joe does it all the time.

Why, just the other day Nancy Pelosi said, "I believe in natural gas as a clean, cheap alternative to fossil fuels."[65] WTF? I'm surrounded by morons. Last time I checked, natural gas is a fossil fuel. But it gets worse. Pelosi was trying to illustrate for the press the need to quickly pass my economic recovery program. That's when the most powerful woman in the world said the damnedest thing—especially since everyone knows the total population of the United States is in the neighborhood of 300 million people . . .

"**Every month** that we do not have an economic recovery package **500 million Americans** lose their jobs."

—Nancy Pelosi[66]

CHAPTER 47

Little White Lies

Don't deny it. All of us—including you—have told little white lies from time to time. Think back to when you were a kid. I bet you told a white lie to keep your dad from kicking your ass because you raided his last Budweiser from the fridge. Or, maybe, to avoid paying higher taxes, you engage in a bit of "creative accounting" and lie about your wages or deductions when April 15 rolls around.

Don't get me wrong. I'm not on your case. In the words of my favorite former CBS anchorman, Dan Rather, "Who among us has not lied about something? . . . I think you can be an honest person and lie about any number of things."[67]

I take comfort in those words. Why? I've told quite a few white lies since becoming president. None of them, however, tops the whopper I told during my first hundred days in office. They say confession is good for the soul, so I guess that's why I'm divulging this secret. But first, I must be clear about something. When *I* tell a white lie it's not for personal gain. Far from it.

It's for the good of the country.

In that respect I should be *thanked* for my nefarious role massaging the truth.

On February 9, 2009, I stood before Congress and the American people and urged them to support my stimulus bill. I knew full well that if my bill was to have a chance in hell of passing, I had to assure Americans that it contained no "earmarks." Otherwise it'd be dead on arrival. There was one problem.

My bill contained *more than nine thousand earmarks*.

That's when I took a calculated risk and told this little white lie . . .

"What it does **not** contain, however, is a single pet project, **not a single earmark,** and it has been stripped of the projects members of both parties found most objectionable."

—Me[68]

CHAPTER 48

Hold Your Fire

Let's face facts. Our Constitution was written exclusively by dead white guys. The lack of a multicultural, multinational panel of authors is reason enough to scrap the thing and start over. Short of that, I think we can begin by shooting down the Second Amendment—which is why I've surrounded myself with a team that has a rich history of taking potshots at gun ownership by private citizens.

Let's start with my veep. Joe bragged that he's "the guy who originally wrote the assault weapons ban."[69] Technically, as you might expect from Joe, that's not fully accurate. Democratic senators Howard Metzenbaum and Dennis DeConcini were faster on the draw and authored bills before Joe. Still, his commitment to disarming the Second Amendment is on target.

Then there's Hillary Clinton, who's been shooting her mouth off about regulating guns for decades. She's one hot pistol, who goes ballistic any time the topic of gun control fires up. She talks a good game, and that's half the battle.

Even Cass Sunstein, my regulatory czar, and a former animal-rights activist, hit the bull's-eye when he told a crowd at Harvard, "We ought to ban hunting, if there isn't a purpose other than sport and fun. That should be against the law."[70]

And while Janet Reno, former U.S. attorney general, isn't on my staff—yet—I like her view that "waiting periods are only a step. Registration is only a step. The prohibition of private firearms is the goal."[71]

The problem with most folks in my administration is that they think that to change the Constitution on gun control they've got to play by the rules. Hogwash. I prefer the way Rahm Emanuel operates . . .

"We're bending the law as far as we can to ban an entirely new class of guns."

—Rahm Emanuel[72]

CHAPTER 49

Bust Reduction

When I began to rule, one of my first acts as president was to ship that damn bust of Winston Churchill back to England. Boy, did Hannity, Limbaugh, and the other wackos on talk radio have a field day with that. If they'd asked me, I would have explained I don't have anything against Churchill. The fact of the matter is that there are simply too many busts in the White House and on Capitol Hill. Everywhere I turn there's another armless bust staring at me.

It's really kinda creepy.

Franklin. Lincoln. Jefferson. Madison. Washington—it's a Who's Who of American history. I bring this up for a reason.

When it comes to busts, Al Gore has got to be the biggest boob to ever work in public office. A senator-turned-vice-president should know the basics of our nation's history. Not Al. He's about as clueless as they come—which is surprising considering that he was raised by a U.S. representative and spent much of his life wandering aimlessly through the halls of Congress. You'd think at some point he would have familiarized himself with our Founding Fathers and former presidents.

Instead, while he and Bill Clinton took a tour of Monticello, the house that President Jefferson designed and had built for himself, then–vice president Gore looked as dazed and confused as ever. As he approached a row of busts of the likes of George Washington and Benjamin Franklin—where faces are about as familiar as McDonald's Golden Arches—nothing registered.

The question Al asked the Monticello curator made me glad Al isn't on my team . . .

"Who are these people?"

—Al Gore[73]

CHAPTER 50

The Anointed One

Ever since I erupted onto the world stage, I've been adored by the masses.

People love me. Yes, people worship the ground—or water—that I walk on.

They can't get enough of me.

And for good reason. I'm a walking stimulus package. My very presence on the scene has sprouted countless homespun industries selling products bearing my likeness. Besides the T-shirts and bumper stickers, there are stacking Obama matryoshka dolls; Obama action figures with guns, swords, and light sabers; Ben & Jerry's "Yes, Pecan!" ice cream; and, given my predilection for waffles, my favorite, Obama Waffles, which promise *Change you can taste*.

And for those who want the ultimate stimulus package, try Obama Condoms.

Now, some detractors and even Democrats are jealous. Harry Reid comes to mind. Poor guy. He's been around Washington for decades and nobody's made even a coffee cup with his mug on it. Others are worried that all of this attention unnecessarily elevates me to messianic status. They gave me hell for my joke during the 2008 Al Smith fund-raising dinner, when I quipped, "Who is Barack Obama? Contrary to the rumors you have heard, I was not born in a manger. I was actually born on Krypton and sent here by my father Jor-El to save the Planet Earth."

I thought it was a funny line. Still, I know I have to be careful with the whole messiah thing. A number of faithful fans actually believe I'm the real deal . . .

"Barack has captured the youth. And he has involved young people in a political process that they didn't care anything about. When the Messiah speaks, the young people will hear, and the Messiah is absolutely speaking."

—Louis Farrakhan, The Nation of Islam[74]

Notes

1. "Obama's minister: U.S. 'No. 1 killer in the world,'" WorldNet Daily.com, 3/14/2008. http://www.wnd.com/index.php?fa=PAGE .view&pageId=58928.

2. "Iraq Brings Nods of Agreement," Jennifer Hunter, Sun-Times Media, 8/20/2007. http://www.suntimes.com/news/politics /obamacommentary/516952,CST-NWS-debate20.stng.

3. "Biden Also Plagiarized, Padded His Resume," E. J. Dionne Jr., *New York Times*, 11/17/1987. http://query.nytimes.com/gst /fullpage.html?res=9B0DE5DD173BF934A2575AC0A961948260& sec=&spon=&pagewanted=all.

4. "All aboard! Obama pals back violent Gaza flotilla," Aaron Klein, WorldNetDaily.com, 5/31/2010. http://www.wnd.com/index.php ?fa=PAGE.view&pageId=160661.

5. "The Greatest Obstacle to Border Enforcement, Part 3," Chuck Norris, Townhall, 6/1/2010. http://townhall.com/columnists /ChuckNorris/2010/06/01/the_greatest_obstacle_to_border _enforcement,_part_3.

6. Ted Rueter, *449 Stupid Things Democrats Have Said* (Kansas City, Mo.: Andrews McMeel Publishing, 2004), 3.

7. "List of Biden's Political Blunders," FOXNews, 6/27/2010. http:// www.foxnews.com/politics/2010/05/25/list-bidens-political -blunders/.

8. "Biden Calls Custard Shop Manager a 'Smartass' After Taxes Comment," FOXNews, 6/27/2010. http://www.foxnews.com/politics

/2010/06/27/biden-calls-custard-shop-manager-smartass-taxes
-comment/.

9. "Despite 9.6% Unemployment Rate, White House Says Economy Stronger Today by 'Virtually Any Measure' Than Two Years Ago," Fred Lucas, CNSNews.com, 9/7/2010. http://cnsnews.com/news /article/72321.

10. "Obama: I'm not 'getting fresh or anything,'" Political Ticker, CNN, 4/10/2008. http://politicalticker.blogs.cnn.com/2008/04/10 /obama-im-not-getting-fresh-or-anything/.

11. "ABC News Shocker: The 'All Time Dumb Quotes' Are All From Republicans," Warner Todd Huston, NewsBusters.org, 1/1/2009. http://newsbusters.org/blogs/warner-todd-huston/2009 /01/01/abc-news-shocker-all-time-dumb-quotes-are-all -republicans#ixzz0yzj9pvOF.

12. "The increasingly erratic, super-gaffetastic Joe Biden," Michelle Malkin, Creators Syndicate, 10/22/2008. http://michellemalkin .com/2008/10/22/the-increasingly-erratic-super-gaffetastic-joe -biden/.

13. "Michelle Obama: 'For the First Time in My Adult Lifetime, I'm Really Proud of My Country,'" Jake Tapper, ABC News, 2/18/2008. http://blogs.abcnews.com/politicalpunch/2008/02/michelle -obam-1.html.

14. "Just How Smart Is Obama?" Victor Volsky, American Thinker, 8/18/2010. http://www.americanthinker.com/2010/08/just_how _smart_is_obama_1.html.

15. "Oh, That Joe! (No. 29 in a Series)—Obama & Biden's Three-Letter Word: J-O-B-S," Jake Tapper, ABC News, 10/15/2008. http:// blogs.abcnews.com/politicalpunch/2008/10/oh-that-joe-n-6 .html.

16. "Clown alert: Janet Napolitano says the 'system worked,'" Michelle Malkin, Michellemalkin.com, 12/27/2009. http://

michellemalkin.com/2009/12/27/clown-alert-janet-napolitano
-says-the-system-worked/.

17. "New Controversial Video Obama's Radical Marxist Pastor: 'Land of the Greed and Home of the Slave,'" Pamela Geller, Atlas Shrugs, 11/2/2009. http://atlasshrugs2000.typepad.com /atlas_shrugs/2009/11/new-controverisal-video-obamas-radical -marxist-pastor-land-of-the-greed-and-home-of-the-slave.html.

18. Video available at: http://www.youtube.com/watch?v=zHflFFK oaNM. Retrieved 9/11/2010.

19. "President Obama blasts lies, disinformation," Glenn Thrush, Poltico, 8/29/2010. http://www.politico.com/news/stories/0810 /41575.html.

20. "Biden living up to his gaffe-prone reputation," John M. Broder, New York Times, 9/11/2008. http://www.nytimes.com/2008/09/11 /world/americas/11iht-biden.4.16081515.html.

21. "Rahm: 'Take Your F***ing Tampon Out,'" Ed Driscoll, Pajamas Media.com, 5/4/2010. http://pajamasmedia.com/eddriscoll/2010 /05/04/rahm-take-your-fing-tampon-out/.

22. "Vice President Gore on CNN's 'Late Edition,'" CNN.com, 3/9/1999. http://www.cnn.com/ALLPOLITICS/stories/1999/03/09 /president.2000/transcript.gore/.

23. "How Could the Obama Administration Have Hired This Guy?" Jack Kelly, Pittsburgh Post-Gazette, 9/13/2009, B3.

24. "Barack Obama Jr: Babies named after the US president," Sue Mitchell, BBC News, 1/18/2010. http://news.bbc.co.uk/2 /hi/8461222.stm.

25. "Lyrics: Songs About President Obama," FOXNews, 9/24/2009. http://www.foxnews.com/politics/2009/09/24/lyrics-songs -president-obama/.

26. "Biden: Pelosi 'most powerful person' in politics," Mike Memoli, The Swamp, Chicago Tribune, 7/19/2010. http://www

.swamppolitics.com/news/politics/blog/2010/07/biden_pelosi
_most_powerful_per.html.

27. "Rep. Hank Johnson: Guam could 'tip over and capsize,'" Christina Wilkie, The Hill, 3/31/2010. http://washingtonscene .thehill.com/in-the-know/36-news/3169-rep-hank-johnson -guam-could-tip-over-and-capsize.

28. "Top Ten Alvin Greene Quotes," Matthew Stoker, Associated Content, 9/3/2010. http://www.associatedcontent.com /article/5756846/top_ten_alvin_greene_quotes.html?cat=60.

29. "Obama: '10,000 People Died' in Kansas Tornado," Associated Press, 5/9/2007. http://www.foxnews.com/story/0,2933,270 852,00.html.

30. "List of Biden's Political Blunders," FOXNews.com, 6/27/2010. http://www.foxnews.com/politics/2010/05/25/list-bidens -political-blunders/.

31. "Reid apologizes for racial remarks about Obama during campaign," Mark Preston, CNN.com, 1/9/2010. http://articles.cnn .com/2010-01-09/politics/obama.reid_1_john-heilemann -african-american-voters-senator-reid?_s=PM:POLITICS.

32. "Harry Reid: 'I had nothing to do with' Unemployment, Foreclosures," Patricia Murphy, Politics Daily, 9/7/2010. http://www .politicsdaily.com/2010/09/07/harry-reid-i-had-nothing-to-do -with-unemployment-foreclosur/.

33. "Rahm: 'Take Your F***ing Tampon Out,'" Ed Driscoll, Pajamas Media.com, 5/4/2010. http://pajamasmedia.com/eddriscoll/2010 /05/04/rahm-take-your-fing-tampon-out/.

34. "Biden Musings on Hillary Clinton," John M. Broder, New York Times, 9/10/2008. http://thecaucus.blogs.nytimes.com/2008/09 /10/biden-musings-on-hillary-clinton/.

35. "Obama 'Special Olympics' Crack On Tonight Show," The

Huffington   Post,   3/19/2009.   http://www.huffingtonpost
.com/2009/03/19/obama-special-olympics-cr_n_177185.html.

36. "Biden's description of Obama draws scrutiny," Xuan Thai and
Ted Barrett, CNN Washington Bureau, 2/9/2007. http://www
.cnn.com/2007/POLITICS/01/31/biden.obama/.

37. "Michelle Obama Gets Personal," Jennifer Parker, ABC News,
9/7/2007. http://abcnews.go.com/Politics/Decision2008/story?id
=3571642&page=1.

38. "Massa Details Naked Shower Fight With 'Son of the Devil's Spawn,'" FOXNews, 3/8/2010. http://www.foxnews.com
/politics/2010/03/08/massa-accuses-democrats-pushing-pass
-health-care/.

39. "Biden: There's 30 Percent Chance We'll Be Wrong," Mark
Hemingway, National Review Online, 2/6/2009. http://www
.nationalreview.com/corner/176938/biden-theres-30-percent
-chance-well-be-wrong/mark-hemingway.

40. "A Terrible Thing to Waste," Jack Rosenthal, New York Times,
7/31/2009. http://www.nytimes.com/2009/08/02/magazine/02F
OB-onlanguage-t.html.

41. "List of Biden's Political Blunders," FOXNews.com, 6/27/2010.
http://www.foxnews.com/politics/2010/05/25/list-bidens
-political-blunders/.

42. "No Regrets for a Love of Explosives; In a Memoir of Sorts, a War
Protester Talks of Life With the Weathermen," Dinitia Smith,
New York Times, 9/11/2001. http://www.nytimes.com/2001/09/11
/books/no-regrets-for-love-explosives-memoir-sorts-war
-protester-talks-life-with.html?pagewanted=1?pagewanted=1.

43. "Pelosi Remarks at the 2010 Legislative Conference for National
Association of Counties," Press Release, Nancy Pelosi, 3/9/2010.
http://www.speaker.gov/newsroom/pressreleases?id=1576.

44. "Pelosi: Health care bill can be bipartisan even without GOP votes," Martina Stewart, CNN, 2/28/2010. http://politicalticker .blogs.cnn.com/2010/02/28/pelosi-health-care-bill-can-be -bipartisan-even-without-gop-votes/?fbid=2iKA-9S_iif.

45. "Obama apologizes to Nancy Reagan for séance quip," Foon Rhee, *Boston Globe*, 11/7/2008. http://www.boston.com/news /politics/politicalintelligence/2008/11/obama_apologize_1.html.

46. Valerie Jarrett, Meet the Press transcript, 11/9/2008. http://www .msnbc.msn.com/id/27629956/.

47. "Biden's description of Obama draws scrutiny," Xuan Thai and Ted Barrett, CNN.com, 2/9/2007. http://www.cnn.com/2007 /POLITICS/01/31/biden.obama/.

48. "The Notorious Blago," Scott Raab, *Esquire*, 1/11/2010. http:// www.esquire.com/features/people-who-matter-2010/rod -blagojevich-interview-0210-3.

49. "The Notorious Blago," Scott Raab, *Esquire*, 1/11/2010. http:// www.esquire.com/features/people-who-matter-2010/rod -blagojevich-interview-0210-3.

50. "Average Joe Has a 'Successful Dump,'" Byron Wolf, ABC News, 8/20/2008. http://blogs.abcnews.com/politicalradar/2008/08 /average-joe-has.html.

51. "Report: Obama said 'I Am a Muslim,'" Pamela Geller, *American Thinker*, 6/16/2010. http://www.americanthinker.com/2010/06 /report_obama_said_i_am_a_musli.html.

52. "Mr. Obama Gaffes Again: 'My Muslim Faith,'" Steve Gilbert, *Sweetness & Light,* 9/7/2008. http://sweetness-light.com/archive /obama-gaffes-again-my-muslim-religion.

53. "Congressman: 'I Don't Worry About the Constitution' on Health Care Overhaul," FOXNews.com, 4/2/2010. http://www .foxnews.com/politics/2010/04/02/democratic-lawmaker-dont -worry-constitution-health-care-overhaul/.

54. "Biden not worried about Southern Dems," Associated Press, 8/28/2006. http://www.msnbc.msn.com/id/14554439/.

55. "Pelosi: Pole vaults and parachutes," Carolyn Lochhead, SFGate .com, 1/28/2010. www.sfgate.com/cgi-bin/blogs/nov05election /detail?entry_id=56238.

56. "Obama Misspeaks, Calls Biden 'The Next President'; Biden Calls Obama 'Barack America,'" ABC News, 8/23/2008. http:// blogs.abcnews.com/politicalradar/2008/08/obama-misspea -1.html.

57. "Barack Obama's gaffe: seeking greater inefficiencies," Amie Parnes, Politico, 7/20/2009. http://www.politico.com/news/stories /0709/25165.html.

58. "Exclusive: Eric Massa on 'Glenn Beck,'" FOX News, 3/10/2010. http://www.foxnews.com/story/0,2933,588685,00.html.

59. "Only ABC Highlights Biden's Gaffe About 'Dead' Mother of Irish PM, Stephanopoulos Lauds VP's 'Smile,'" Scott Whitlock, Newsbusters.org, 3/18/2010. http://newsbusters.org/blogs/scott -whitlock/2010/03/18/only-abc-highlights-bidens-gaffe-about -dead-mother-irish-pm-stephano#ixzz0z3xddx00.

60. Ron Bloom, "Czar Ron Bloom Agrees With Mao," Address at an Investor Conference, YouTube.com, posted 9/12/2009 at www .youtube.com/watch?v=RCvQ8BSUv-g.

61. "Obama's Science Czar on His Past Work: 'If You Read It and You Have a Problem, You're Misreading It,'" Nicholas Bal- lasy, CNSNews.com, 6/14/2010. www.cnsnews.com/news/article /67690.

62. "No Regrets for a Love Of Explosives; In a Memoir of Sorts, a War Protester Talks of Life With the Weathermen," Dinitia Smith, New York Times, 9/11/2001. http://query.nytimes.com/gst /fullpage.html?res=9F02E1DE1438F932A2575AC0A9679C8B63.

63. "Vice President Biden visiting Denver to talk about the

middle class," Kevin Host, Examiner.com, 5/25/2009. http://www
.examiner.com/republican-in-denver/vice-president-biden
-visiting-denver-to-talk-about-the-middle-class.

64. "Biden to limit role of vice president," Mike Allen, Politco, 12/6/08.
http://www.politico.com/news/stories/1208/16261.html.

65. "Nancy Pelosi Doesn't Know That Natural Gas Is a Fossil Fuel,"
Rush Limbaugh, 8/25/2008. http://www.rushlimbaugh.com
/home/daily/site_082508/content/01125111.guest.html.

66. "Pelosi's 500-million-person Slip," Clemente Lisi, New York Post,
2/4/2009. http://www.nypost.com/p/news/politics/item_gPtx1N
2ZYl5nU7DOLSjOGO;jsessionid=AE2F41355B430BD81CC78CB19
E3D9BE0.

67. "JournoList Member Advocates Lying to Public," Ed Driscoll,
PajamasMedia.com, 8/13/2010. http://pajamasmedia.com
/eddriscoll/2010/08/13/journolist-member-advocates-lying/.

68. "Obama's Press Conference Transcript," Barack Obama, Real
Clear Politics, 2/9/2009. http://www.realclearpolitics.com
/articles/2009/02/obama_press_conference_transcript.html.

69. "Joe Biden: The Voice Of Anti-Gun Experience," NRA-ILA,
9/5/2008. http://www.nraila.org/Legislation/Read.aspx?ID=4160.

70. "The Gathering Storm Over Guns," Wayne LaPierre, Human
Events, 5/1/2009. http://www.humanevents.com/article.php?id
=31679.

71. "Bearing arms still a fundamental right," Steve Skutnik, Iowa
State Daily, 10/23/2002.

72. "The Gathering Storm Over Guns," Wayne LaPierre, Human
Events, 5/1/2009. http://www.humanevents.com/article.php?id
=31679.

73. "Which vice president is the king of gaffes?" Tim Graham,
BNET, 3/23/1999. http://findarticles.com/p/articles/mi_qa3827
/is_199904/ai_n8836395/.

74. "Farrakhan addresses world at Saviours' Day 2008," Askia Muhammad, *The Final Call*, 3/5/2008. http://www.finalcall.com /artman/publish/National_News_2/Farrakhan_addresses _world_at_Saviours_Day_2008_4427.shtml.